There are several variations of paper folding. The most commonly known is the Japanese art of origami, which lets you create elaborate three-dimensional objects such as flowers and animal figures from squares of paper.

Tea bag folding, first developed by Tiny van der Plas of Holland, uses the decorative paper packets that European tea bags come in and has become enormously popular. When combined, folded tea bag packets create unique designs which may be used to embellish greeting cards or other paper art.

When scrapbookers Laura Lees and Kris Mason discovered this paper-folding technique, they saw endless possibilities for scrapbook embellishment. And while American tea bag packets aren't as attractive as those in Europe, there are many other printed papers available. Kris and Laura both have started companies that provide papers specifically for this wonderful craft. Presented here are only a few of the innumerable opportunities for using paper squares to add three-dimensional flair to your scrapbook pages.

page 16

page 19

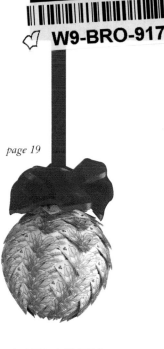

MEMORY
M A K E R S

MEMORY FOLDING™

*Add dimension to your scrapbook
pages with this unique paper art*

page 30

Copyright ©1999 Satellite Press
475 W. 115th Avenue, #6
Denver, CO 80234
303.452.1968 Fax 303.452.2164
www.memorymakersmagazine.com

Satellite Press is home of *Memory Makers*®, a magazine dedicated to educating and inspiring scrapbook and paper artists. Call 1.800.366.6465 to subscribe or for more information.

ISBN 1-892127-06-7

Paper

We recommend the use of archival quality, photo-safe paper and other supplies for your scrapbooks. Lightweight paper folds easier than heavy, but cardstock can work well for large projects. While there are papers designed specifically for folding (see Sources on page 32), you may also experiment with specialty papers such as vellum, doilies, and wrapping and tissue papers. Two-sided paper may be somewhat difficult to find, but it increases your creative options, and papers with repeating patterns can really enhance your designs.

Paper Tips

• Create your own patterned paper with stamps, paints, or punches.
• If you just have to use a particular paper that is one-sided and you really need two-sided, use two pieces back-to-back for each fold.
• To change the size of the opening in an open design, either change the size of the paper square or the number of pieces.
• Use extra squares of paper to embellish scrapbook pages.

Symbols

PAPER EDGE

FOLD

DIRECTION of fold

PINCH

CUT

PATTERN SIDE of paper

REVERSE SIDE of paper

Methods

It is important to be precise when cutting paper for folding. The more exact your beginning square or triangle, the better the folded piece. Use a metal-edged ruler and craft knife and measure carefully before cutting.

Take the time to practice before using your chosen paper. If you're new to folding, try using larger squares until you feel comfortable with the process.

Use a metal straight edge and craft knife to cut paper into squares.

Terms

Corner mount Any finished folded piece used to mount photographs to a page.

Closed wreath Eight folded pieces that meet at the center to create an embellishment without a center opening.

Open wreath Eight or more folded pieces combined to create an embellishment with a center opening for a photograph or journaling.

Frame Any number of folded pieces combined in varied shapes, i.e., hearts or rectangles, to form a frame for a photograph or journaling.

Border Any number of folded pieces combined and used to outline or accent a page.

Tools

- Craft knife
- Ruler
- Cutting mat
- Scissors (regular and decorative)
- Circle template
- Adhesives
    splits
    photo tape
    liquid glue
    glue sticks
- Accessories for embellishment
    paper punches
    pens
    stickers
    stamps

TRIANGLE FOLD OPEN WREATH
eight 2 ½" squares

garrett & marissa

summer 1999

take time to stop and smell the flowers

THE TRIANGLE FOLD is used as the basis for many other folds that follow. Here it is used to create an open wreath for framing a photograph. For a closed wreath, follow assembly for open wreath, but make the closed points of the triangles meet in the center. Both projects use the Yellow Daisy Specialty Folding Paper, included in this book.

TRIANGLE FOLD CLOSED WREATH
eight 2 ½" squares

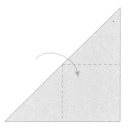

TRIANGLE FOLD

1. With pattern side facing up, fold C and D to A and B, and crease.

2. Open flat, fold A and C to B and D, and crease.

3. Open flat and turn paper over with pattern side down.

4. Bring A to D, forming a triangle, and crease.

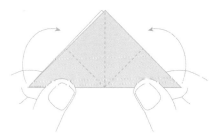

5. Open flat, fold C to B, forming a triangle, and crease.

6. Holding folded corners in either hand, push fingers toward center, as shown below. Move the flap in your left hand toward the back and bring flap in your right hand forward, forming a layered triangle.

For Step 6, hold the folded corners in either hand and push fingers toward center to form a layered triangle.

ASSEMBLY

▶ **Holding two triangles with closed points facing same direction, slide top flap of one triangle between two flaps of the other triangle.**

▶ **Snug them up tightly so the point is flush with the long edge.**

▶ **Secure with adhesive.**

Repeat with remaining triangles, sliding first triangle into last to finish.

SINGLE STAIR CLOSED WREATH
eight 3" squares
CORNER MOUNTS
four 1½" squares

Having a Ball at... Garrett's 1st birthday

SINGLE STAIR FOLD Follow Steps 1 to 6 of Triangle Fold (page 5).

7. With closed point at bottom, fold top right flap down along center line and crease.

8. Bring folded flap from right to left.

THE SINGLE STAIR FOLD is a variation of the triangle fold — as with other folds that follow, you begin with the triangle fold and add steps. Here it is used to create closed wreaths and corner mounts. The closed wreath is 3-dimensional when not pressed between the pages of a book. For corner mounts, simply use one piece for each corner.

GIFT DECORATION
eight 2" squares

CARD
eight 2" squares

ASSEMBLY

▶ Holding two pieces with closed points facing same direction, slide single flap of one triangle between two flaps of the other triangle.
▶ Snug them up tightly so that the bottom points meet.
▶ Secure with adhesive on back of single flap of inserted piece.

Repeat with remaining triangles, sliding first triangle into last to finish.

KITE FOLD OPEN WREATH
seventeen 3 ½" squares of vellum

THE KITE FOLD is another variation of the triangle fold — as with other folds that follow, you begin with the triangle fold and add steps. Here it is used to create a unique wreath that enhances floral photographs and journaling. The kite fold is also used in combination with the triangle fold to create a whimsical border as shown at right — the green paper is folded with the triangle fold described on page 5 for the kite bottoms.

ASSEMBLY

▸ Holding two pieces with closed points facing same direction, slide one piece into space between kite and flap of other piece.

▸ Snug pieces up so that the closed point of the inserted kite is near the center of other kite.

▸ Secure with adhesive on the wing of the bottom piece.

Repeat with remaining pieces, sliding first piece into last to finish.

   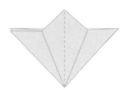 

KITE FOLD Follow Steps 1 to 6 of Triangle Fold (page 5).

7. Bring top right flap perpendicular to center fold.

8. Use a pencil to open the edges of raised flap.

9. Keeping center creases aligned, remove the pencil and press flat, creasing both sides of the new "kite" shape.

10. Turn piece over.

11. Repeat Step 7.

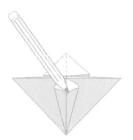

12. Repeat Step 8.

13. Repeat Step 9.

KITE FOLD BORDER
   five 3" squares of floral paper
   five 1" squares of green paper folded with triangle fold for kite bottoms

THE TRIANGLE FLOWER FOLD

is another variation of the triangle fold. As you can see, it is a very versatile fold. You can use it to create large pinwheel pieces as shown at right, or to make a light border of individual buds as shown on the following page.

TRIANGLE FLOWER BOUQUET
four 3" squares, eight 2½" squares, two 2" squares, five 1½" squares

TRIANGLE FLOWER FOLD Follow Steps 1 to 6 of Triangle Fold (page 5).

7. Bring top right flap to left side.

8. Fold remaining right flap down along center line and crease.

9. Bring top left flap to right side.

10. Mark a point approximately ¼ total length away from bottom closed point.

Cut small strip of green paper with decorative scissors.

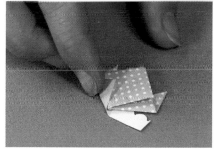

Strips should be approximately ¼" x 1¼".

"Wrap" the strip around base of flower as shown, bringing ends to back and securing with adhesive.

TRIANGLE FLOWER BORDER

sixteen 2" squares and plain green paper for flower bases, vine, and leaves

11. Fold top edge of right flap down to mark and crease.

12. Bring top left flap to right side.

13. Fold remaining left flap down along center line and crease.

14. Bring top right flap to left side.

15. Fold top edge of left flap down to ¼ length mark as for right and crease.

THE POINTED PETAL CORNER FOLD is a great one to use for experimenting with paper positioning. Simply by holding your specialty or patterned paper one way or another before you begin the fold, you will end up with very different looks. This project uses the Apple Specialty Folding Paper included in this book. The icon next to the wreath indicates how the piece should look after completing steps 1-6 of the Triangle Fold.

By beginning with the apple in this position you get a totally different look from the same fold.

POINTED PETAL CORNER OPEN WREATH
eight 2½" squares

POINTED PETAL CORNER FOLD
Follow Steps 1 to 6 of Triangle
Fold (page 5).

7. Bring top right flap to left side.

8. Fold top left flap down along center line and crease.

9. Slide finger between remaining left flaps.

The apple uses twenty-five 2" squares folded on the diagonal into triangles, and then folded again in half to form smaller triangles. Starting from the bottom, pieces are pinned to a 2 1/2" Styrofoam ball and topped with silk leaves and a stem cut from corrugated brown paper.

10. Bring top left flaps to right side.

For this wreath, we folded the paper beginning with the apple right side up in the triangle.

11. Fold top right flap down along center line and crease.

ASSEMBLY

▶ **Holding two pieces with closed points facing same direction, place flap of one piece into space between flap and diamond of the other.**

▶ **Snug pieces up so that the long open end of inserted piece is flush with edge of diamond of other piece.**

▶ **Secure with adhesive.**

Repeat with remaining pieces, sliding first piece into last to finish.

Here the apple is oriented upside down.

12. Bring top right flap to left side.

GIFT CARD
eight 2 ½" squares

PEEK-A-BOO CARD
twelve 1½" squares

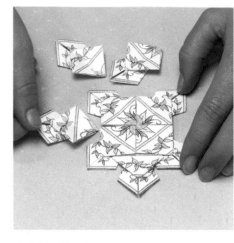

ASSEMBLY

▸ Position four folded pieces so that their lower diamonds form a center square and the petals radiate out.
▸ Slide a new folded piece between two others so that the lower diamond of the new piece lays under the other two and is inserted as far as possible.
▸ Secure with adhesive.

Continue in this manner with remaining three folded pieces.

POINTED PETAL FOLD
Follow Steps 1 to 6 of Triangle Fold (page 5).

7. Bring top right flap to left side.

8. Fold bottom edge of right flap up along center line and crease.

9. Fold top edge of left flap down along center line and crease.

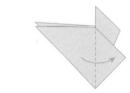

10. Bring top left flap to right side.

11. Slide finger between remaining left flaps.

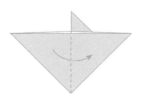

12. Bring top left flap to right side.

13. Fold bottom edge of left flap up along center line and crease.

14. Fold top edge of right flap down along center line and crease.

15. Bring top right flap to left side.

THE POINTED PETAL FOLD looks more elaborate than others in this book, but is just as easy to create. And like others, it is an extension of the basic triangle fold. Linking petals together in a circle makes the peek-a-boo card on the previous page and the open wreath shown here. You'll need to draw a 5¾" circle template to assemble the large wreath. The closed wreath on the gift card takes on a whole new look and can be made with the Vine Specialty Folding Paper, included in this book.

POINTED PETAL OPEN WREATH
sixteen 2½" squares

ASSEMBLY

▸ Draw a 5¾" circle guide.
▸ Holding two pieces with closed points facing same direction, place bottom of one piece into the petal of other piece.
▸ Snug up so that pieces are as tight as possible while following circle guide.
▸ Secure with adhesive on back of inserted piece.

Repeat with remaining pieces, shaping to circle guide, and sliding first piece into last to finish.

POINTED PETAL CONNECTOR FRAME
twenty-two 3" squares—
twelve pointed petal folds (see page 15);
ten pointed petal connectors

Lois and Marcia Volk
Mother and Daughter
~1940~

POINTED PETAL CONNECTORS can be used to create square and rectangular frames with the additon of diamond-shaped connectors. The connectors make the symmetrical assembly possible, facing the pointed petal folded pieces in opposite directions. Here the connectors have also been used to square off the corners of the frame.

POINTED PETAL CONNECTOR FOLD Follow Steps 1 to 6 of Triangle Fold (page 5).

7. Bring top right flap to left side.

8. Fold top edge of right flap down along center line and crease.

9. Fold top edge of left flap down along center line and crease.

10. Bring top left flap to right side.

11. Slide finger between remaining left flaps.

MEMORY MAKERS

MEMORY FOLDING™

Specialty Folding Paper For Your Scrapbooks

POINSETTIA

ACID FREE, ARCHIVAL QUALITY

VINE

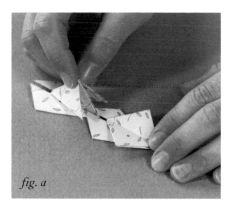

fig. a

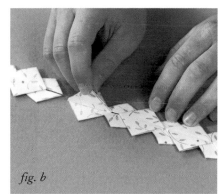

fig. b

fig. c

fig. e

fig. c

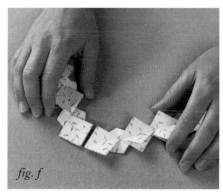

fig. d

fig. g

fig. f

ASSEMBLY

The frame is assembled in four pieces—two vertical and two horizontal. The vertical strips each have four pointed petal pieces and one connector. The horizontal strips each have two pointed petal pieces and two connectors.

VERTICAL ASSEMBLY *(make two)*

▸ Lay two pointed petal pieces next to each other with petals pointing to your right.
▸ Pinch together the diamond of the right piece, bringing the flaps perpendicular to the table.
▸ Slide the point of the right piece between the petals of the left piece *(fig. a)* as far is it will go.
▸ Unpinch and open the diamond.
   Repeat with two more pointed petal pieces.

▸ Lay two assembled sets next to each other with the petals pointing to the center.
▸ Slide the points of the connector between the petals of both sets as far as they will go *(fig. b)*.
▸ Unpinch and flatten the diamond.

HORIZONTAL ASSEMBLY *(make two)*

▸ Snip a small channel approximately ⅜" deep into the point of one connector *(fig. c)*.
▸ Pinch together the diamond of a second connector, bringing the flaps perpendicular to the table.
▸ Slide the point of the second connector into the channel of the first as far as it will go *(fig. d)*.
▸ Unpinch and flatten the diamond.
▸ Using the pinch and slide method, connect one pointed petal piece to each side of the double connector *(fig. e)*.

FRAME ASSEMBLY

▸ Lay the strips down to form corners and secure with adhesive *(fig. f)*.
▸ To accent corners, angle a connector under two corner pieces and secure with adhesive *(fig. g)*.

12. Bring top left flap to right side.

13. Fold top edge of right flap down along center line and crease.

14. Fold top edge of left flap down along center line and crease.

15. Bring top right flap to left side.

DIAMOND FOLD OPEN WREATH
eight 2½" squares

THE DIAMOND FOLD

can look detailed and intricate when done in a patterned paper that can be cut to shape. First follow the steps for the diamond fold, then follow design lines of the paper to create a custom-shaped wreath. This design uses the Poinsettia Specialty Folding Paper, included in this book. Paper positioning (see page 12) is key here so that you end up with leaves in the right corner of each folded piece.

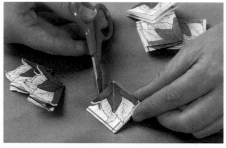

ASSEMBLY

▸ **Trim folded diamonds along design lines as shown. Or if you prefer, you may assemble the wreath and then trim the outer edges.**

▸ **Holding two pieces with closed points facing same direction, place top flap of one piece between flaps of other piece.**

▸ **Snug pieces up so that the closed point of upper piece is approximately ½ of the way down the edge of inserted piece.**

▸ **Secure with adhesive.**

Repeat with remaining pieces, forming a circle and sliding first piece into last to finish.

DIAMOND FOLD

1. With pattern side facing, fold D to A to form a triangle and crease.

2. Open flat, fold C to B to form a triangle and crease.

3. Open flat and turn paper over with pattern side down.

4. Fold A and C to B and D and crease

5. Open flat, fold C and D to A and B and crease.

6. Holding folded edge with both hands at bottom near V-shaped crease, push fingers toward center, forming layered diamond shape. Press flat.

**POINTED PETAL CORNER
ORNAMENT** eight 2" squares.
Follow folding instructions
on page 12. Assemble pieces
snugged up so there is no
center opening. Add a
bell and tassel, attach
a cord for hanging.

SINGLE STAIR ORNAMENT eight 2"
squares. Follow folding and assembly
instructions on pages 6 and 7. Embellish
with gold pen and mount to gold
paper. Attach three strips of
curled paper in cen-
ter and a cord
for hanging.

ROUND ORNAMENT
twenty-five 2" squares.
Assemble as for apple on
page 13 and attach
a bow and
a cord for
hanging.

**DIAMOND
FOLD OPEN
WREATH**
eight 2 ½" squares.
Assemble as for
wreath on page
18 and attach a cord
for hanging.

DIAMOND FOLD SNOWFLAKE
eight 2 ½" squares. Fold
squares with diamond fold
(page 18) and use a snow-
flake template (see sources
on page 32) to trim.
Assemble as for open
wreath but snug
pieces up so there is no
center opening. Attach a
cord for hanging.

ROUND ORNAMENT
twenty-five 2" squares. Assemble
as for apple on page 13 and attach
a bow and cord for hanging.

THE WINGED DIAMOND FOLD is enhanced with fancy edges by punching the corners of your paper squares before you fold them. The beginning steps for the winged diamond fold are almost the same as those for the diamond fold on page 18, but one step is skipped to eliminate the crease down the center front of the piece. "Wings" are then pulled from the diamond.

WINGED DIAMOND OPEN WREATH
twelve 4" squares

WINGED DIAMOND FOLD

1. With pattern side facing up, fold D to A to form a triangle and crease.

2. Open flat and turn paper over with pattern side down.

3. Fold A and C to B and D and crease.

4. Open flat, fold C and D to A and B and crease.

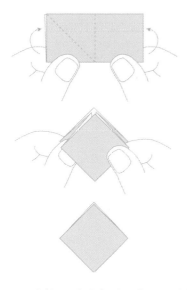

Punch the corners of your squares before folding. For further embellishment, punch a diamond shape in front and back corners and line with contrasting paper.

5. Holding folded edge with both hands at bottom near V-shaped crease, push fingers toward center, forming layered diamond shape. Press flat.

6. Holding diamond with closed point at bottom, grasp top of inside right flap (2 layers), bring it forward and down so that the folded edge meets the lower outside edge, forming a "wing," and crease.

7. Repeat Step 6 on left side.

8. Fold the upper point of top diamond so that it lines up with wings as shown and crease.

ASSEMBLY

▸ Draw a 4" circle template.
▸ Holding two pieces with closed points facing same direction, slide the closed point of one piece between wing and back of other piece.
▸ Snug up so that the inserted piece is about halfway into other piece and at an angle while following circle template and allowing point of back piece to be seen.
▸ Secure with adhesive.

Repeat with remaining pieces, forming a circle and sliding first piece into last to finish.

FOLD BACK
OPEN WREATH
eight 8" x 4" rectangles folded into 4" squares

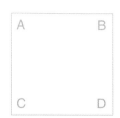

FOLD BACK

1. With pattern side down, fold C and D to A and B and pinch edge to mark center. Do not crease.

2. Open flat.

3. Fold C and D to center mark and crease.

4. Turn piece over so that pattern side is up and fold is at top.

5. Fold bottom left corner up to top edge and crease.

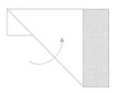

6. Fold corner back to lower folded edge and crease.

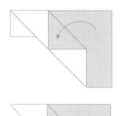

7. Use scissors to snip off or fold to the back the small triangle at top left.

THE FOLD BACK is most attractive when the paper square is the same on both sides. The easiest way to achieve this is to fold a rectangle in half to make a two-sided square. The half fold back on the next page uses one-sided paper and a variation of the fold back.

ASSEMBLY

▶ **Holding two folded pieces, place one piece over the other, lining up lower edge of top piece with edge of bottom piece.**

▶ **Snug up so that the tip of folded back triangle of top piece is aligned with the corner of bottom piece. (Adjust this positioning for a smaller or larger opening.)**

▶ **Secure with adhesive.**

Repeat with remaining 7 pieces, forming an inner octagon and placing the first piece over the last to finish.

HALF FOLD
BACK

1. With pattern side down, fold C and D to A and B and crease.

2. Fold lower left corner up to top edge and crease.

3. Fold corner back to lower folded edge and crease.

ASSEMBLY

▶ Holding two pieces, place one piece over the other, lining up lower edge of top piece with the edge bottom piece.

▶ Snug up so that the tip of the fold back triangle of top piece is aligned with corner of bottom piece. (Adjust this positioning for a smaller or larger opening.)

▶ Secure with adhesive.

Repeat with remaining 7 pieces, forming an inner octagon and placing the first piece over the last to finish.

▶ For the closed wreath, follow steps for open assembly but snug up so that the lower corners of both pieces are aligned.

HALF FOLD BACK
OPEN AND CLOSED WREATHS
eight 2 ½" squares

JACKET FOLD FRAME
eighteen 4" squares of vellum

ASSEMBLY

▶ Hold one piece vertically with folded edge to the left; hold another piece horizontally with folded edge to the top.
▶ Slide one piece between the fold and the flat back of other piece.
▶ Snug up so that the pieces join at a right angle and the corners meet.
▶ Secure with adhesive between the flat backs of the pieces.
▶ Slide the next piece between the fold and the flat back of the horizontal piece.
▶ Snug up so that the lower corners of the center triangles meet.
▶ Secure with adhesive between the flat backs of the pieces.

Continue in this manner, forming rectangle, and sliding last piece into first to finish.

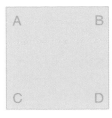

JACKET FOLD

THE JACKET FOLD is simple yet dramatic. Create different looks by varying the size and number of squares used. Here we show a small square frame using four 3" squares, a medium rectangle frame using six 6" squares, and a large frame using eighteen 4" squares (page 24).

1. With pattern side up, fold A and B to C and D and crease.

2. Fold top layer of bottom right corner up to top edge and crease.

3. Fold top layer of bottom left corner up to top edge and crease.

4. Fold left point back to folded edge and crease.

5. Fold right point back to folded edge and crease.

6. Fold bottom point up to top edge and crease.

JACKET FOLD FRAME
four 3" squares for small square;
six 6" squares for large rectangle

Assembly for square Jacket Fold Frame: Proceed as outlined for rectangular frame (page 24) but omit the extra pieces between corners—the square uses only four pieces.

V Fold Heart-Shaped Frame
seventeen 3" squares

THE V FOLD can be used to make many different borders and frames. Here we've shaped the folds around a heart-shaped template and made a pocket page for keepsakes. You can create varied looks with this fold by using one- or two-sided paper (two-sided is used here), and by using the front or backside of the folded piece as the "up" side.

V FOLD

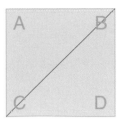

1. Cut squares in half diagonally to form two triangles.

2. Place triangle pattern side up.

3. Fold B to C to form a smaller triangle but do not crease.

4. Pinch point to mark center.

5. Open flat with pattern side up.

6. Fold top point down to center mark and crease.

7. Turn piece over so pattern side is up and fold is at the top.

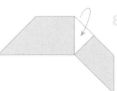

8. Fold upper right point down to center mark and crease.

9. Fold upper left point down to center mark and crease. This fold looks good from both sides, so you may choose either one for the front.

ASSEMBLY

Follow the inner edge of heart template and secure each folded piece to template with adhesive as it is added. Work from the center down one side to the bottom, then the other.

▸ Place one piece at top point of heart template as shown.
▸ Add a piece to the side by sliding it between the previous piece and the template.
▸ Snug up so that the lower point of the new piece is aligned with side point of diamond of previous piece.
▸ Adjust angle as needed to follow template.

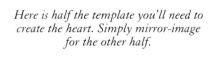

Here is half the template you'll need to create the heart. Simply mirror-image for the other half.

WAVY TRIANGLE FOLD FRAME
thirteen 3½" squares

NOW THAT YOU'VE GOT THE
BASICS of paper folding down, it's time to expand its use. The very basic triangle fold takes on a whole new look when part of it is cut away in a wavy pattern. Use the template provided or create a whole new look with your own cutting line.

Simply cut the top of your folded triangle for a whole new look.

ASSEMBLY

▶ Holding two cut-away triangles with closed points facing same direction, slide front of one triangle between two flaps of other triangle.
▶ Snug them up so inserted triangle is into the other as far as it can go and flaps overlap as shown.
▶ Secure with adhesive.

Repeat with remaining triangles, sliding first triangle into last to finish.

WOVEN STAR CUT-AWAY

Follow Steps 1 to 6 of Triangle Fold (page 5). On triangle made from 3" squares, mark 1" up from closed point on both sides. Use a ruler to make a straight line connecting the marks and cut along this line. The lower closed piece may be used as a corner mount; use the large strip to create the woven star.

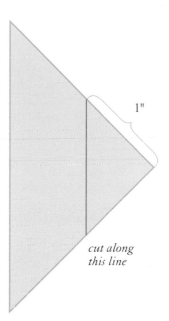

1"

cut along this line

A WOVEN ASSEMBLY is another way to completely change the look of the basic triangle fold. Here the bottom portion of the triangle folds are cut away and the tops are interwoven to create multicolored stars. You may use the bottom cut-aways as corner mounts.

WOVEN STAR
four 3" squares for each motif

ASSEMBLY

- ▶ Hold one cut piece horizontally, with long side at top.
- ▶ Hold second cut piece with long side at right.
- ▶ Slide top flap of first piece into back opening of other piece.
- ▶ Snug up so that pieces are as close together as possible and form a right angle.
- ▶ Secure with adhesive on back of right piece.

Repeat with two remaining pieces, placing back flap of last piece between two open flaps of first piece.

Mr. & Mrs. Jacob Grasl, 1900

happy Mothers Day

ALMOST EVERY
DAY EACH SUMMER
WE GO TO CHANNEL
ISLANDS BEACH.
THE WATERS ARE
SO GENTLE THERE
WE CALL IT BABY
BEACH.

IT IS A
WONDERFUL
PLACE TO
SPEND THE
DAY WITH
FAMILY.

There is no limit to what you can do with interesting paper and a few simple folds. Scrapbook embellishments, picture frames, greeting cards, candleholders, and even a mobile are easily created using the folds outlined in this book. See page 32 for the specific folds used for these projects.

FOLDS USED FOR GALLERY PIECES
(pages 30-31)

1. Closed wreaths–kite, triangle, fold back, diamond, single stair, diamond wing folds. Open wreath–V fold.
2. Open and closed wreaths–diamond fold trimmed to form snowflakes.
3. Woven star cut-away.
4. Open wreath–kite fold.
5. Open wreath–fold back.
6. Closed wreath–diamond fold.
7. Open wreath–variation of V fold.
8. Open wreath–kite fold. Closed wreaths–V fold, fold back. Embellishments–pointed petal, triangle flower folds.
9. Open wreath–single stair fold.

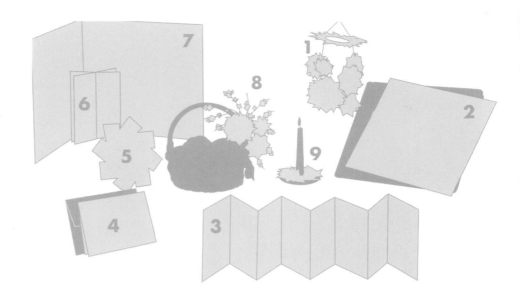

PAPERS USED IN THIS BOOK CAME FROM THE FOLLOWING SOURCES

▶ **FOLDED MEMORIES**
23632 Highway 99 #F135
Edmonds, WA 98026-9206
Phone 425-673-7422
Fax 425-673-9422
e-mail krismason@foldedmemories.com
www.foldedmemories.com
pages 4-5, 12-13, 14, 18, 19 and 23.

▶ **FRANCES MEYER, INC.**
(wholesale only)
PO Box 3088
Savannah, GA 31402
800-372-6237
pages 6-7, 16 and 22.

▶ **HOT OFF THE PRESS**
1250 N.W. Third
Canby, OR 97013
503-266-9102
pages 11, 25 and 29.

▶ **JUDI KINS**
17803 Harvard Boulevard
Gardena, CA 90248
310-515-1115
page 24

▶ **KANGAROO AND JOEY**
15410 S. 17th Lane
Phoenix, AZ 85045
602-460-4841
page 8

▶ **L PAPER DESIGNS**
7909 207th Place SW
Edmonds, WA 98026
425-775-9636 (voice and fax)
e-mail lpaper@telisphere.com
www.kapplerusa.com/lpaper.htm
page 15

▶ **PAPER ADVENTURES**
PO Box 04393
Milwaukee, WI 53204-0393
800-727-0699
page 26

▶ **THE PAPER PATCH**
(wholesale only)
PO Box 414
Riverton, UT 84065
801-253-3018
page 10

▶ **PROVO CRAFT**
285 East 900 South
Provo, UT 84606
800-937-7686
page 25

Other sources

▶ **MAKE YOUR OWN SNOWFLAKES**
New York: Scholastic Inc., 1996
page 19

PHOTO CREDITS

Front cover and page 8, Laura Lees
Page 9, Erica Pierovich
Page 15, Fowler Photography, Edmonds, WA
Page 20, Connie Miden Cox
Page 25, KIDS Photography, Edmonds, WA
Page 29, Maria V. Landry
Pages 30-31,
    3. Susan Walker
    4. Karen Gerbrandt
    5. Nicole King
    7. Kristi Winter